Congratulations on taking your first step toward food independence.

When we sat down and tackled this idea we had three objectives:

1. How can we teach people to affordably grow healthy produce?
2. How can we create a system that resolves the climate constraints people face?
3. What are the space constraints some people will have and how can we solve that?

After going through all of these different scenarios, spending hours on research, interviewing experts, and even building multiple samples mimicking the types of situations you might face, we've come up with this guide "The 4 Foot Farm Blueprint".

This guide is designed to show you how to grow clean, fresh, non-GMO fruits and vegetables for you and your family while saving a bundle of money in the process. If you choose to utilize this guide to turn a profit, we even offer a blueprint with profit maximization in mind (we'll touch on this in the selling/bartering chapter). For space saving and extreme climate situations, we will break down indoor growing opportunities using vertical gardening principles. For creating abundant yields of diversified food, we will show you how to efficiently grow outside. Both will concentrate on maximizing productivity of a small space in order to make the blueprint accessible to as many people as possible.

Putting these two opportunities into play year round will create an extremely abundant yield that will allow you and your family to substantially lower your grocery bill and improve your health by by increasing your consumption of fresh fruits and vegetables.

Before you start diving into the content of the guide, there is one very important piece of advice that you should keep in mind - **DO NOT GET OVERWHELMED!** If you are new to growing your own food or you have never grown anything using some of these methods, always remember this one simple fact, growing edible plants is something incredibly simple that humans have been doing for thousands of years. Being a gardener is something that is encoded into our DNA.

TABLE OF CONTENTS

CHAPTER 1: THE PLAN
Planning your indoor and outdoor garden

Every good garden starts with a plan and goals. Our indoor and outdoor gardens are no exception.

While what we are growing indoors and outdoors will be different, we will have the same general goals - maximize the advantages we have in both environments to produce a variety of produce for personal consumption, sale or trade. We will get into the options of what to do with your produce later, but for now let's lay out a plan for your two new gardens.

Indoor Garden Planning

Before we talk about seeds and the schedule for growing, we want to discuss what to grow, and why. In this indoor vertical garden, we will be focused mainly on harvesting from plants while they are in a vegetative state. In other words, we are not growing any plants to produce roots, fruits, seeds or flowers. Instead, we will focus on growing plants that produce nutritionally diverse and flavorful greens and herbs that you will be able to harvest throughout the year.

With that in mind, and assuming you build your indoor wall to the same specifications that we will lay out step-by-step, you will have a total of 384 spaces to plant on the garden wall. The planting grid in Table 2 will show you where each plant will go. You will not want to plant all of the plants at the same time because it will crowd the roots in the growing medium. You also don't want to plant the same kind of plants too close together because this can cause stress in the plants when the roots of two of the same annuals meet. It is for this reason that we recommend you plant 3 successions of 128 plants into the wall.

We recommend the following combination of plants for your first planting:

Table 1

Name of Plant	Number of Plants	Estimated Yield Per Plant in Ounces	Estimated Total Yield in Pounds	Days to Harvest	Harvest Window Length in Days
Spinach	32	6	12	60	60
Green Lettuce	32	4	8	50	70
Red Lettuce	16	4	4	50	70
Kale	32	8	16	45	75
Parsley	4	4	1	75	45
Basil	4	4	1	60	60
Mizuna	4	4	1	45	75
Arugula	4	4	1	45	75

** Based on this example, each harvest should yield 44 lbs of food.

There are many other types of greens that you could include and experiment with. This is dependent on what your end goal for your produce is as (Eat, Barter, Sell?).

In my home, my current garden is growing mostly herbs that I will be harvesting for sale.

If you want to try to grow some different plants other than what we suggest above, you could also try some of the following:

- Collard Greens
- Swiss Chard
- Bok Choi
- Tatsoi
- Sorrel
- Purslane
- Komatsuna

We recommended the greens and herbs in table 1 because they are the most commonly grown garden greens and therefore the ones you are most likely to know and eat in your day to day diet. If you have adventurous taste buds, by all means, try some of the more unusual greens out there.

Planting Calendar

The planting schedule will be pretty simple.

That is one of the great things about indoor growing, there is no need to wait for good weather to break before you get started.

On Day 1 of Week 1, you will plant the first planting of 128 plants by following the green pattern shown in table 2, below.

The next planting will be on Day 120 or Week 16, whichever is easier for you to keep track of on your calendar. This is the pattern highlighted in blue on the table.

Then finally, the third planting will take place on Day 240 or Week 32. For this planting, follow the yellow pattern on the table. It is as simple as that.

Once the new plants have germinated and have begun to establish themselves, you will harvest/kill the previous planting from the garden wall to prevent stress in the plants. Another thing that you could do, if you wish, is start the plants in just the rockwool plugs and then once they germinate, you could add them to the wall. You could also keep track of your germination rates from the first planting and stagger the planting dates of the plants for the second planting to get as close to germinating on Day 120 or during week 16 as possible. This would reduce the lull of a few weeks that will result from going from the first planting to the second as well as from the second to the third. Although, you will be kill/harvesting all of the remaining vegetation from the first planting once the second planting germinates, which is going to give you a large amount of greens to work with for a period of time.

Table 2

L = Lettuce,   K = Kale,   P = Parsley,   S = Spinach

B = Basil,   M = Mizuna,   A = Arugula

* Grey = First Planting (Day 1 - 119),
* Black = Second Planting (Day 120 -239)
* White = Third Planting (Day 240 - 365)

Outdoor Garden Planning

The needs for an outdoor garden are a little different, because you will be depending at least partially on mother nature for access to the big three; water, food and light. It is for this reason that you will want to start by finding where the best placement is for your garden.

LIGHT

When you are thinking about where to place your garden, you want to think about two things, water drainage and hours of direct sunlight available. The rule of thumb is that you want to place your garden in an open spot that gets at least six hours of sunlight. The more hours of sunlight you can get, the better your plants will do.

When looking for the "sunny spots", also remember that the sun changes its position in the sky throughout the year. Because of this, the best placement is typically where your garden has full southern exposure. This means there will be nothing shading the spot as the sun dips down on the southern horizon in the fall or slowly works its way back up in the sky in the spring. If you don't have a spot that gets a full six hours of sun, place your garden in an area that gets the most sunlight during afternoon hours. This typically works best for annual growing.

SLOPE

It's easier to wet dry soil than to dry out overly saturated soil.

Because of that, you want to plant your garden away from an area where water pools during heavy rains. If there are any low-lying areas in your yard, steer clear of them as moisture will be a problem for you. Even if you are building a raised bed, you don't want to put it in a low-lying area. A lot of garden problems stem from either too much or too little water.

SCHEDULE

Once you've picked out your optimum spot where you're going to plant, we can talk a little bit about what you will be planting.

Since you are growing strictly greens and herbs indoors, the outdoor garden will be focused on growing roots, fruits, flowers and seeds that will be a good nutritional complement to the indoor-grown greens.

In the outdoor garden, since we will be working with 16 square feet (a 4' by 4' area), it is a good idea to manage the garden in 16 separate one square foot blocks. Keep in mind that just because we are growing outdoors, it does not mean that we need to rule out using some vertical growing techniques. These techniques really help maximize the small spaces to create abundant yields. For example, on the north side of the garden, you could put in garden towers (A build guide is included in Appendix F) to increase the overall space you have available. For simplicities sake, we will focus this grow plan on just the 16 blocks.

The following times are based on a garden in Zone 6B. The first planting is roughly 15 days before the last frost of the spring and the last planting is 6 weeks before the first frost of the fall. The length of your growing season may differ, you can use this website to find out about when to start your garden: http://www.garden.org/zipzone/

Table 3 (North is the top row)

NORTH

4/1: Carrots/ Radish 6/1: Tomato 9/1: Peas	4/15: Carrots/ Radish 7/1:Tomato	4/1: Carrots/ Radish 6/1: Tomato 9/1: Peas	4/15: Carrots/ Radish 7/1:Tomato
4/1: Broccoli 5/1: Peas 7/15:Kohlrabi 9/15: Beets/ Radishes	4/1: Broccoli 5/1: Peas	4/1: Broccoli 6/1: Beans 7/15: Cucumber 9/15: Turnip/ Radish	4/1: Cabbage 7/15: Carrot/ Radish
4/1: Onions 6/1: Squash 7/1: Broccoli	4/1: Onions 5/1: Peas 7/15: Broccoli	4/1: Onions 7/15: Cucumber 9/15: Beets/ Radish	4/1: Cabbage 7/15: Carrot/ Radish

| 4/1: Peas
5/1: Squash
7/1: Pepper | 4/1: Beets/
Radish
5/1: Beans
6/15: Pepper | 4/1: Beets/Radish
5/1: Beans
6/15: Pepper | 4/1:Radish
4/15:
Artichoke
7/1: Pepper |

SOUTH

Planting Calendar

1/1: Start Indoors: Onions

3/1: Start Indoors: Broccoli, Cabbage, Artichoke

4/1: Plant Beets, Carrots, Radishes and Peas. Transplant Onions, Broccoli and Cabbage

4/15: Start Indoors: Tomatoes and Peppers. Plant Carrots and Radishes. Transplant Artichoke

5/1: Start Indoors: Tomatoes. Plant Peas, Beans, Squash

6/1: Plant Beans and Squash. Start Broccoli in a pot

6/15: Transplant Tomatoes and Peppers

7/1: Transplant Broccoli, Peppers, Tomatoes

7/15: Transplant Broccoli. Plant Carrots and Radishes

9/1: Plant Peas

9/15: Plant Beets, Turnips and Radishes.

Table 4 - Yield Totals

Name of Plant	Number of Plants	Estimated Yield Per Plant in Pounds	Estimated Total Yield in Pounds	Days to Harvest	Harvest Window Length in Days
Tomatoes	4	10	40	60-80	90+
Peppers	4	2	8	90	75+
Carrots	216	1/12	18	75	1
Beets	64	¼	16	55	1

Broccoli	5	1½	8	60-70	30
Cabbage	2	5	10	80	1
Squash	2	8	16	55	45
Cucumbers	2	5	10	55	45
Beans	3 squares	2	6	60	30
Peas	6 squares	1	6	55	40
Kohlrabi	9	2/3	6	60	1
Onions	108	1/6	18	120-180	1
Turnips	16	¼	4	50	1
Radishes	12 squares	2	24	25-35	1

Based on these estimated yields, you will be able to harvest 190 lbs of produce from just a 4' by 4' plot. If you were so inclined, you could also alter this plan to focus in on just the items that produce most bountifully for you and you could easily grow upwards of 300 lbs of produce in one growing season under optimal conditions. For those of you who enjoy year round growing weather you could grow over 1000 lbs of food from this outdoor plan.

CHAPTER 3 - PLANTING BASICS
What every gardener should know about growing

When picking out where to put your Since we're going to be focusing on both indoor and outdoor growing lets go over some basics that we feel you should know.

Indoor Gardening - Vertical Garden using hydroponic principles

The indoor garden that we're going to be putting together is based on Patric Blanc, a French Botanist who became popular by introducing wall gardens to urban architecture.

Benefits/Issues to Growing Indoors

- You control the temperature, light and amount of water and nutrients the plants receive in a soil-less growing medium. No more drought, flood, or soil disease concerns.

- You are away from the scrutiny of others. If God forbid there was an uprising, you're food supply has been out of the watchful eye of potential looters.

- The vertical garden means less bending. For some folks constant bending can cause some serious wear and tear on the body.

- You don't have to worry about outdoor pests, and you don't have to worry about your garden dying because a neighbor "treats" their yard.

Yield-Boosting Techniques - Companion Planting & Succession Planting

When we researched how best to manage growing in such small spaces, we kept coming across two basic gardening concepts, companion planting and succession planting. Both ideas are very simple, but sometimes overlooked by gardeners who are mimicking large farming techniques. Most large modern farms, organic or otherwise, follow steps that are harmful to nature around them in many ways. Instead of following Big Ag's mistakes, we will mimic nature to increase our yield.

Companion Planting Basics

Some plants can occupy the same space relatively harmoniously with others. Gardeners that take advantage of that fact are using companion planting. You may remember from our promotional video there was a secret called "stalk stacking" which is another term for companion planting. In the illustration to the left, perhaps one of the most well known companion planting techniques is shown. Known as "three sisters," Corn, Squash, and Pole Beans can all be planted together at the same time. Each plant matures at different stages and the plants benefit from one another. The squash provide a living mulch so that the corn can out compete the weeds. The corn gives the beans something to grow up on while also shading the squash plants from mid-summer sun. The beans will also take nitrogen from the atmosphere and fix it to tiny colonies of bacteria on their roots so that it is available to other plants.

Though you won't be using the three sisters technique in your indoor gardens, the principles will be the same. The plants that we recommend in our layouts take advantage of companion planting whenever it is possible, which will help each different type of plant to flourish. As you continue gardening, you can refer back to this companion planting graphic that will help you identify which plants can go together most advantageously.

Companion Planting Chart

Plant	Good Companion	Bad Companion
Beans, Peas	Beet, Cabbbage, Cucumber	Onion, Fennel, Garlic

Beets	Cabbage, Onion, Lettuce	
Broccoli, Cabbage, Cauliflower, Kale	Potato, Beet, Celery, Onion,	Tomato, Pepper, Bean
Carrots	Chive, Lettuce, Pea, Radish	Fennel, Cabbage
Lettuce	Bean, Carrot, Cucumber	Celery, Parsley
Onions, Garlic	Beet, Cabbage, Carrot, Lettuce, Tomato	Pea, Bean, Parsley
Peppers	Basil, Carrot, Onion	Bean, Cabbage, Kale
Potato	Bean, Cabbage	Cucumber, Squash, Tomato
Spinach	Bean, Pea	
Tomato	Basil, Onion, Parsley, Celery	Potato, Fennel, Cabbage

Succession Planting Basics

Did you know if you were to dig up the soil in your yard and have it analyzed, you would find out that there are a large numbers of seeds in it?

When plants release their seeds, they inevitably end up on the existing soil where they are covered with decaying matter which turns to soil. Perennial rooted plants will thrive and most of the annual seeds in the soil will lie dormant for years in undisturbed areas. But, anytime a human or animal pulls up a plant from the dirt, hundreds of annual and perennial seeds alike are exposed and some of them will sprout and grow in the space that was made as a result of the disturbance.

This is the natural demonstration of succession planting, as soon as there is space to grow, something will grow there. As a gardener, you have control over what will grow next in your garden and that is why you will plant in successions throughout the season.

A common mistake made by first time gardeners is that gardening is something that you do in the spring and then harvest from in the fall. While it is possible to simply plant and then come back and harvest when the produce is ready, this method isn't the most efficient use of your gardens, particularly if you are growing in small spaces.

The fact is a productive garden, which is a garden with successive plantings, is being planted and harvested throughout the growing season. This is the main reason that the time tables are laid out for you for both gardens. Successive plantings in both the indoor and outdoor garden are the key to supplying you with not only increased overall yield, but also a wider variety of vegetables than would be possible from a single planting in such a small space.

Food, Water and Light

It doesn't get any more basic than this.

These are the three things that all plants need to survive and thrive. With the garden wall, the great thing is that you can automate most of your work. Timers for the lights and water pump are inexpensive and effective at keeping your plants on the right track. If you have a large enough reservoir, you won't have to add water and liquid fertilizer more than once a week.

Your Plants Need Food Too!

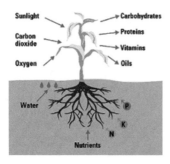

Plants access nutrients mainly using their root system. The necessary nutrients and the soil bacteria that transform them into usable materials have to be available in your garden soil in order for your plants to thrive in your outdoor garden.

You can perform a soil test to make sure all

necessary nutrients are at the appropriate levels at the beginning of your growing season. In your hydroponic system, all nutrients have to be steadily supplied to the root structure of the plant in order for the plant to grow at a healthy rate.

In the vertical garden we will be using liquid fertilizer to provide the necessary nutrients. We recommend using a company named General Hydroponics for your liquid fertilizer.

There are three main ingredients in fertilizer that all assist the plants in different ways:

Abbr.	Element	Function
N	Nitrogen	Responsible for green growth (vegetation) of plants, helps plant to defend against pests, assists in photosynthesis
P	Phosphorous	Aids in distribution of energy throughout plant, needed for strong root growth
K	Potassium	Strengthens plant metabolism and aids in water distribution throughout plant

Water

It's pretty simple… Make sure to water your plants. They need to stay hydrated just like any other living organism would need to stay hydrated.

For the indoor garden, make sure to refill your reservoir once a week with new water and fertilizer. There is no need to drain the reservoir at any time because the same dilution (or similar levels) of fertilizer and water will still be in the tank at the end of the week, just a smaller amount of it.

In your outdoor garden, let mother nature do as much of the watering as possible as it is the best water for your garden. When you need to water, do so in the morning or early afternoon so that any excess water can evaporate before night falls. This will prevent many soil fungi from thriving.

Always try to use the purest water source you have available. In most cases, this will mean using rainwater or well water. Municipal tap water has chemicals in it like chlorine and fluoride which are not beneficial to plants. If you live in a state where they allow you to capture rainwater, do it... then use it to water your plants.

Light

With our indoor gardens this is our greatest concern.

In some cases growing indoors can be problematic once the plants "size up". However,

in our project the calendar will keep you rotating out plants after about 16 weeks to avoid this. Keeping life spans short and continually harvesting will reduce the need to feed large amounts of foliage on a single plant. Keep in mind that with artificial light, the closer you get it to the plant, the more effective it will be.

For your outdoor garden, you will want to put your garden in the sunniest spot possible and you must place it where it receives at least 6 hours of sun. Afternoon sun is more beneficial for annual vegetables than morning sun, so lean that way if you must pick between one or the other.

CHAPTER 3 - FINDING SEEDS
Dirt cheap tricks to finding seeds for your garden

There is something really wonderful about growing plants from seed to harvest. Sometimes, it will be so easy for you, you will feel like you are stealing the food right from the ground. Those are the good gardening years that will make you really love growing your own food. But, looking through seed catalogs and seeing some of the high prices some companies are asking for seed takes the fun out of your harvest no matter how large or small. The thing is, it doesn't have to be that way - especially for gardens the size of the indoor and outdoor gardens that we're working with in this guide.

That's why we're going to quickly cover some of your money saving options when it comes to seeds.

Seed Options That Will Save You A Bundle!

1. Seed Savers Exchange - This is a group based out of Iowa that connects heirloom growers from around the world. Their annual yearbook publication has over 10,000 heirloom varieties of fruits, vegetables, flowers and trees listed. There is a small annual membership fee, but it is a great way to connect with other gardeners and farmers from around the world and find something new and interesting to grow.

   One thing to note, they offer a discounted rate for low-income people that want to join. For more information you can go here http://www.seedsavers.org/Membership/

2. GardenWeb Seed Exchange - This is a message board where you can list seeds you want or scroll through to look at seeds people have listed to share. This exchange service is an interesting way

to get access to a wide variety of seeds without having to pay the annual membership fee. Hundreds of varieties are listed on there for the cost of a self addressed stamped envelope.

For more information go here: http://forums2.gardenweb.com/forums/exseed/

3. Local Gardening Groups and Clubs - This would be the best starting point if getting free seeds is your number one goal. Not only will you have access to lots of different types of seeds that were locally saved, you will also get to talk to other local gardeners and exchange ideas. There are a couple of gardening groups in my area that have annual seed swaps where folks get together and trade seed. If you show up and you are new, you will leave with more seed than you know what to do with.

The best way to locate these groups is by taking advantage of the interwebs. Search for Facebook groups, meetups on Meetup.com, or try a general search for "[Your City] Gardening Groups", "[Your City] Seed Exchange", etc... You get the picture.

Most importantly, be resourceful. When you're looking for free seeds that is your best asset.

Self Reliance Seed Club

Of course we have to do a soft push for Crisis Education's very own Self Reliance Seed Club. You could find cheaper seeds using some of the methods above, but here's the thing. The seeds in the monthly kits are especially chosen based on the small gardening methods we're showing you within this guide... We're basically holding your hand and eliminating the potential losses from guesswork you'll be doing should you try seed hunting on your own.

For more information (And the "backdoor" member's only special) to the Self Reliance Seed Club go here: http://www.crisiseducation.com/srscreport

Bonus Tip: The Seed Journal

The most important thing that you can do in regard to seeds is to keep track of your experiences with the seeds that you are using. Below is a basic template for you to use in your journal. If you're old school like myself, I keep this in a little black notebook. My good friend Mike (That helped me put together this guide) is a little more computer savvy and he uses an excel spreadsheet.

Keeping a journal will help you with your future grows. It's a road map for what's worked and what hasn't worked so well in past endeavors.

(plant name) (seed variety) (seed source)

(date started) (date of first/last germination) (germination rate)

(number of plants) (grown indoors/outdoors)

(date harvest began/ended/total harvest days)

(yield)

(misc. notes)

CHAPTER 4 - THE "LAZY FOOD" METHOD
Reap the rewards while someone else does all the work!

For some of us the idea of becoming more self reliant over our food supply sounds fantastic. However, limitations due to physical ability, time, or lack of resources impedes our ability to ever really do this.Considering this, we tested a theory that we like to call "**The Lazy Food Method**".

Essentially, we posted an ad to Craigslist advertising the need for help with a small garden (See Below).

CL > austin > all gigs > domestic gigs

Reply   rghhc-4234550292@gigs.craigslist.org   flag : miscategorized prohibited spam best of   Posted: less than a minute ago

Need someone to help with small garden (Austin)

I'm looking for someone to assist me with the creation with a small garden. I'm providing all necessary equipment necessary to get project going but I'm seeking someone that is will to do the minimal lifting and assembling.

This is probably just a couple hours per week of maintenance after initial setup (Which should take less than one day).

I'm willing to compensate monetarily however I'd love to split the yield from the garden as compensation. Essentially, I'll front all the necessary collateral and the space and you'll assist me with the assembly and maintenance... we'll split the yield 50/50.

- Location: Austin
- do NOT contact me with unsolicited services or offers
- Compensation: See post for pay

Posting ID: 4234550292   Posted: less than a minute ago   email to a friend

**Feel free to rip-off this template word for word

Responses rolled in within just minutes of the posting. Now, if you are familiar with Craigslist than you know not all of the responses will be what you're looking for, however, we did receive multiple responses that would have been a great fit for the project.

Here is one below:

**Please always use caution when using or meeting people off of Craigslist

The lazy food method itself is quite simple. Find someone that is willing to do whatever it is that you don't want to do. Then compensate them either financially or through the yield of the produce (your choice).

You should be able to hand them the step-by-step instructions from this guide and have them follow it without a problem.

BONUS: Supply Saver Secret

In the first example (above) you'll see where it's stated that we'll be providing all of the equipment necessary. Now, it's easy for you to go online to Amazon and purchase all of the necessary equipment and have it shipped to your home within just a couple days. That truly would be "The Lazy Food Method". However, if you're willing to sacrifice just a little bit of time for a cash savings, look at these deals we were able to pull up in just a few seconds of searching our local Craigslist:

CL > austin > all for sale / wanted > farm & garden - by owner

Reply kr6qb-4159516682@sale.craigslist.org [?]   flag [?] : miscategorized prohibited spam best of   Posted: about a month ago

☆ **STEEL BINS FOR FALL CONTAINER GARDENING - $20 (Burnet, Texas)**

Solid metal bins that came out of an Austin warehouse demolition that are perfect for container gardening or multiple other uses. We have two size
Both are four feet long and 24 " across. The larger of the two is 12" deep and the smaller is 6" deep. There are 4 small holes in the bottom but mor

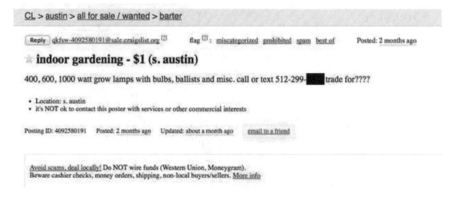

CL > austin > all for sale / wanted > barter

Reply qkfsw-4092580191@sale.craigslist.org [?]   flag [?] : miscategorized prohibited spam best of   Posted: 2 months ago

☆ **indoor gardening - $1 (s. austin)**

400, 600, 1000 watt grow lamps with bulbs, ballists and misc. call or text 512-299-■■■ trade for????

- Location: s. austin
- it's NOT ok to contact this poster with services or other commercial interests

Posting ID: 4092580191   Posted: 2 months ago   Updated: about a month ago   email to a friend

Avoid scams, deal locally! Do NOT wire funds (Western Union, Moneygram).
Beware cashier checks, money orders, shipping, non-local buyers/sellers. More info

It's up to you, time or money. But we simply want to show you that you can really get started with a garden for (financially) next to nothing.

CHAPTER 5: TRICKS OF THE TRADE
How to use your yield to barter or sell for profit

Turning your yield into a tidy profit

If you decide to sell produce locally, you will learn one thing very quickly, demand is almost always greater than supply. Fact is, you have a huge advantage because you are now a part of the local food movement and people will proudly pay you a premium for your produce compared to food costs in grocery stores.

Should you choose to make a little money from your gardening efforts here are some quick tips:

Step 1 - Recon

The first step you should take, if you have the time to do so, is to go to farmer's markets in your area. Toward the end of the day, go around to the different vendors and take note of which items are sold out. Keep a list, as these are the items that you are going to want to focus on selling. Even if you are not selling at the farmer's market yourself, you will see what people buy the most. Farmer's markets are also a great place to get price ranges for your area. Armed with this information, you will be able to create a growing plan tailored toward selling the produce.

Step 2 - Find Buyers

We have already said it before, but it bears repeating, there are not many things easier to sell these days than local produce. However, if the goal is to maximize profits and minimize work, due to the size of garden you'll be working with, we recommend that you focus on selling to one of two types of organizations: locally-owned restaurants that feature lots of local produce or locally-owned grocers that sell mainly local produce. Now that doesn't mean you couldn't sell to your neighbors. I know for me, I get a lot of satisfaction knowing that I supply my neighborhood with healthy greens.

The best way to line up a deal with one of these two types of businesses is to get in touch with a manager. In our guide "The Small Garden Money Map" we dive deeper into how to go about doing this and even supply you with a template and communication script. If you're already a member of the Self Reliance Report you have access to this guide now and can access it at anytime.

Step 3 - Make a New Garden Plan

Throughout the guide we've been focused on growing a variety of foods for home consumption. Now you will need a new garden plan focused on profit. While the results of your information from your local markets may take you in a different direction, given the sizes and space available in your gardens, we recommend that you grow the following items as they are in high demand in most local markets nationwide:

Indoors:
- Flat Leaf (Italian) Parsley
- Genovese (Green, Large leaf) Basil

These culinary herbs can be grown indoors year round and will also be in demand throughout the year with local chefs.

Outdoors:
- **Salad Greens** - Trying to decide what would make the most sense to grow outdoors for sale in such a small spot is difficult, but based on experiences in local markets, a mixture of baby greens would most likely offer the most potential for return.

These greens mature much faster than other potential items that may command a premium price. One other advantageous aspect of these greens is that you can start them very early in the season and change the make-up as the weather heats up.

Garden Profits Planting Calendars

Indoors:

Day 1: Plant 64 parsley plants and 64 basil plants, 8 plants in each row, two spaces between each plant(first succession planting)

Day 70: Plant second succession planting filling in the first of the two spaces

Day 120: Kill harvest first succession to decrease competition with the second

Day 190: Plant third succession planting filling in the second of the two spaces

Day 240: Kill harvest the second succession

Day 310: Plant first succession of year two.

Outdoors:

3/15: Russian Kale 5/15: Green Lettuce 8/1: Spinach	3/15: Red Mustard 5/15: Green Lettuce 8/1: Grn Beet Green	3/15: Green Mizuna 5/15: Green Lettuce 8/1: Red Beet Green	3/15: Tatsoi 5/15: Red Lettuce 8/1: Arugula
4/1: Green Lettuce 5/1: Russian Kale 8/1: Green Lettuce	4/1: Green Lettuce 5/1: Red Mustard 8/1: Green Lettuce	4/1: Green Lettuce 5/1: Green Mizuna 8/1: Green Lettuce	4/1: Red Lettuce 5/1: Tatsoi 8/1: Red Lettuce
3/15: Spinach 5/15: Green Lettuce 8/1: Russian Kale	4/1: Grn Beet Green 5/15: Green Lettuce 8/1: Red Mustard	4/1: Red Beet Green 5/15: Green Lettuce 8/1: Green Mizuna	4/1: Arugula 5/15: Red Lettuce 8/1:Tatsoi
4/1: Green Lettuce 5/1: Spinach 8/1: Green Lettuce	4/1: Green Lettuce 5/15: Grn Beet Green 8/1: Green Lettuce	4/1: Green Lettuce 5/15: Rd Beet Green 8/1: Green Lettuce	4/1: Red Lettuce 5/15: Arugula 8/1: Green Lettuce

Based on this plan, you could anticipate over $1,500 in sales your first year. This is a decent supplemental income based on the minimal work that goes into it. Also, remember that you're working with a small space here. If you decide to do so, you could easily increase your garden size and sales. We have known 1st year growers who have made over $10,000 in sales their first season.

Barter

Understandably everyone that reads this is not a vegan.

Once you have your gardens up and running you will not be able to eat all of the wonderful produce that you're producing. That's why bartering some of your surplus for other dietary necessities is a great way to get cut cost on your overall grocery bill.

Maybe you have a neighbor interested in keeping bees. Maybe there is a local family raising chickens for eggs. Most likely, if you do a simple Craigslist search in your surrounding area you will find someone looking to sell or barter some of their surplus as well.

Welcome to the barter economy. See if you can find somebody that has too much of something that you want. Deer meat is an excellent example in the winter, people literally give the stuff away they have so much of it.

Once you find them, ask if they would be interested in working out a trade for some of your excess produce. If you find you are producing way more greens from your garden wall than you can eat, find someone that is raising hens and see if they would be willing to work out a weekly swap of your produce for their eggs. If you find that no one wants to trade you for your produce, look into making salsa, pickles or jellies for trade instead. These are known as value-added items and often attract more attention than fresh produce in local markets.

As mentioned earlier, gardening is embedded in our DNA. Well, trading with people in our community is too. Bartering for goods has been a currency used since the beginning of mankind. You may not have ever traded anything in your life, but once you do, you will feel how enjoyable it is to produce something and trade it to someone else that is in need of it.

CONCLUSION

Reading this should have given you the knowledge you need to get started today. The only obstacle is getting started, and you're in complete control of that. Remember, be resourceful... You can save a bundle of money on the needed equipment scouring the internet and websites like Craigslist.

Here are the step by step plans to get your garden(s) started today (You can find them in them in the members area for immediate download):

APPENDIX A:

Step By Step Indoor Hydroponic Garden Wall

Part 1 - Materials Lists

Hardware Store List

2 - 80" 2x4 boards (any wood is ok, cedar is ideal if you can get it)

2 - 48" 1x4 cedar planks

Scrap wood to make feet for the 80" boards

4 - 52" 1x2 cedar planks

1 - 52" x 80" sheet of black plastic

1 - 80" length of snow fence

1 - large plastic tub

1 - 48" length of gutter

2 - gutter end caps

1 box drywall screws

2 - 48" T-12, 2 bulb fixtures

4 - 48" T-12 Daylight/Full-Spectrum/6500k bulbs

Hydroponic Supplies

1 - 10' section ½" tubing

1 - 50' roll of ¼" tubing (if you can, buy less, like 5')

1 - hole punch

1 - package ¼" barbed connectors, 10 count

1 - package ¼" drip heads, 10 count

1 - Ecoplus 1056 water pump

1 - Hydrofarm TM01015 timer

3 - Sheets of Grodan 2" starter plugs (50 on each sheet)

2 Yards of Nufoam 24" wide, 2" thick

General Hydroponics Liquid Fertilizer (Bottle A and B)

Part 2 - Step by Step Assembly

Step 1: Measure and cut the 1x4's and 2x4's as follows. Once cut, 1x4's will sit on the 45 degree cuts on the 2x4's. 2x4's will be 80" from outer end to outer end.

1x4's will be 48" from inner end to inner end.

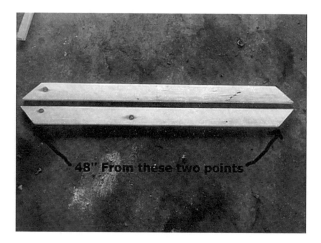

48" From these two points

Step 2: Cut 1 - 52" 1x2 cedar board and 2 - 48" 1x2 cedar board

Step 3: Cut a piece of black plastic 80" x 52" Cut snow fencing so that you have 16x24 rectangles. Cut the 3 yards of nu-foam in half length wise so that you have two pieces that are around 54"x24".

Step 4: Between the 1x4's, lay the black plastic, then the nufoam pieces, side by side, then the snow fencing between the 1x4's.

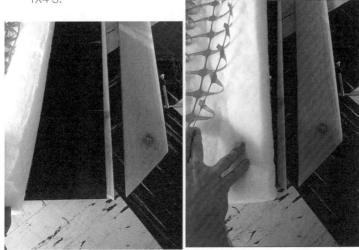

Step 5: Drive in screws along both the top and bottom. While I did this, I used clamps as well as brute force to compress the boards as close together as possible. Leave the heads of the screws along the lower edge sticking out slightly from the front side of the 1x4 so that you can hang the tubing from them.

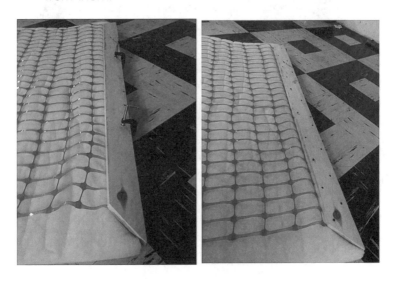

Step 5a: Trim away extra nufoam from the sides so that your 1x4's will sit flush on the 2x4's.

Step 6: Use 1x2's to brace the frame along the back of the frame as shown in the photo below

Step 7: Attach the side boards to the top 1x4's. The 1x4's with the nufoam compressed between them will be wider than your 2x4's. When you screw it all together, assure you are doing so at such an angle that you are going through wood on both the 1x4's and 2x4's. You could also use another piece of scrap wood at each corner to shore it up if you prefer. I pre-drilled my screw holes to avoid splitting the wood.

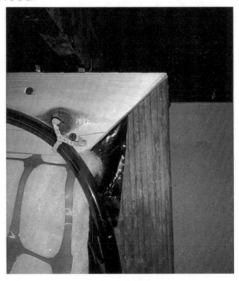

Step 8: Attach the feet to the side boards (any scrap wood for this will do as long as they are at least 12" in length. Drive 2 screws through each footboard.

Step 9: Position the plastic tub under the garden wall.

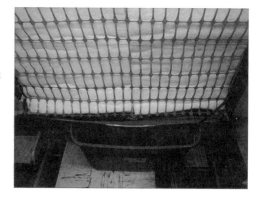

Step 10: Cut away grooves in each side of the tub so that the gutter sits evenly on the tub.

Step 11: lay the black plastic into the gutter, leave a couple inches in the gutter and cut away excess black plastic, grow mat and snow fence.

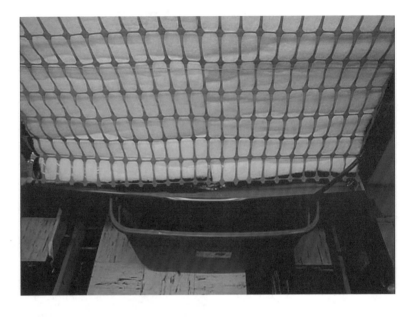

Step 12: Drill holes in the bottom of the gutter so water drips down into reservoir. You can drill as many holes as you wish, but the water will be cycling through slowly so you won't need many holes.

Step 13: Position the pump in the tub and run tubing up the side of the wall and across the top. Use whatever material you have handy to connect the tube to the screw heads we left protruding from the front 1x4.

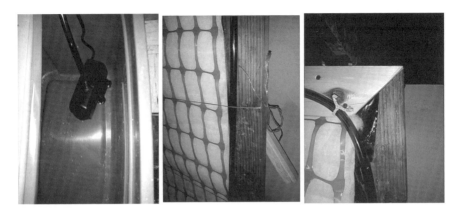

Step 14: Attach drippers to top hose, 6" apart. Make sure that the drippers are in contact with the mats.

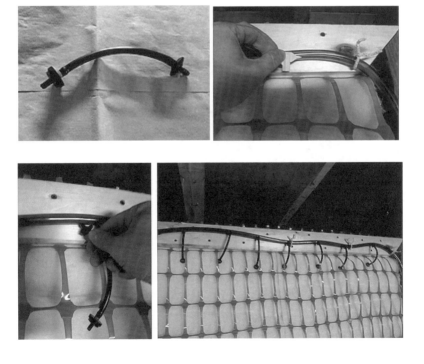

Step 15:

Insert the "first planting" of rockwool plugs following the pattern laid out in Chapter 1 of this guide. Double check to make sure that the rockwool plugs are coming into contact with the mats. You want them to be pushed into the mat, but not too far, because you don't want to reduce the overall depth of the space the roots have to grow.

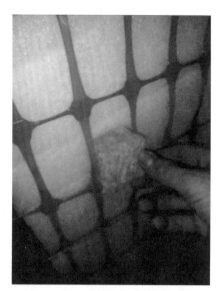

Step 16:

The final step is to run a piece of twine across each row of rockwool plugs. The reason I did this is to make sure that they keep in contact with the grow mats.

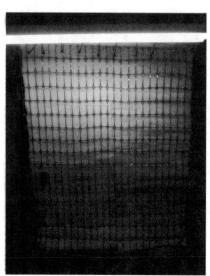

You have now completely assembled the grow wall. The next step is to set up your lighting.

If you have extra space available, I have two recommendations. First, cover the space around the lights with emergency blankets. They are highly reflective and will ensure that as much of your artificial light is making it onto the wall. I also recommend positioning the lights about one foot from the wall so that you are achieving the maximum number of foot candles possible from the fixtures. The lights I purchased from Lowe's came with chains to hang them. I hung one lamp at the length of the chain using the hooks that were included. In order to focus the light on the wall, I ran a piece of twine along the inside of the upper lip on the lamp so that the lamp was angled toward the wall. For the other lamp, I used the chains provided along with an 18" piece of twine on each side. I then ran another piece of twine inside of the upper lip on this lamp as well. I was able to install the hooks directly into exposed floor joists in my basement. If you are anchoring to drywall, install a plastic molly into the drywall first. The lamps aren't heavy, but it is better to be safe than sorry.

Part 3 - Basic Operation

Fill the reservoir and activate the pump. Make sure that there are no leaks anywhere in your tubing. If you find any leaks, a lot of times if you just move the hose around a little it will stop leaking. If you have a persistent leak, you can remove the piece from the blue hose and try to wrap it in teflon plumber's tape to seal it. Because this system is indoors, you want to make sure you don't have any leaks. You also want to check it on a regular basis.

Getting Started

If you have the means to do so, you may want to germinate the seeds in the rock wool plugs before you plant them on the wall. This would be particularly good if you have a heat mat available. Don't go out and buy a heat mat for only this purpose as it isn't necessary, it just helps.

If you don't have anywhere else to germinate the rock wool plugs, go ahead and put them on the wall but do not activate the pump yet. Running the pump at regular intervals will make everything too wet. Instead, dunk the rock wool plugs in water for a second to soak it and then just check it daily to see if you need to add more water. If they are starting to feel dry, go ahead and run the pump for 15 minutes to soak the wall and make water available to the rock wool plugs.

APPENDIX B:

Step By Step to the plastic bottle wall garden
(Low Cost Alternative)

The Plastic Bottle Garden Build Guide

*Please note, you can use this system indoors with some minor alterations (a trough of some kind at the bottom to catch water). You could rig up a self watering system, which would be expensive, or you could just hand water the plants on the top row as often as necessary to keep the soil moist. This would be a far cheaper system than the grow wall, but it won't be as productive (yield wise) as the grow wall.

Materials Used:
- 1 Sheet of Plywood
- 12 2 Liter Bottles
- 48 16.9 oz water bottles
- 60 screws
- newspaper
- soil mix

In the construction of your plastic bottle garden, the containers can vary based on what you have in your waste stream or can get ahold of for free. You might have to buy the sheet of plywood, or you might be able to scrounge one up. Construction site dumpsters are a gold mine for such items. If you have a wooden fence, that will work quite well also. What you're going for is a cheap solution that will hold up through a year. That really only leaves the screws. In this case, I had a bunch of drywall screws left over from a previous project and I used those. They are the black screws and they are pretty cheap.

Step 1 - Prepare the bottles

You want to cut the bottoms off of the bottles and rinse them out, particularly the soda bottles. Once you have the bottoms removed, cut a piece out of one side of the bottle like the picture to the left. The reason you want to do this is because this will give the plant room to grow out from the container. Repeat this process with the smaller water bottles as well.

Step 2 - Prepare the caps

In the photo from step 1, you can see the cap from the two liter bottle has a screw driven through it that is acting as a washer between the screw head and the side of the bottle. The reason I encourage you to do this is because if you do not, I am afraid the plastic will not hold the weight of the plant as the course of the year goes on. Using the cap will hopefully spread out the weight of the plant and soil mix across enough of the surface of the plastic that it holds up through the season. I do not expect these bottles to last for more than 1 year.

Step 3 - Mount the bottles starting on each side and working your way in and down

Using this method will allow you to keep things as evenly spaced as possible without having to spend any time measuring things in advance. If you are using plywood like in the picture, this will also allow you to keep all of the bottles lined up so that excess water will drain into the container beneath it.

Step 4 - Fill the mounted containers with soil mix.

In order to do this, you will need to wad up a piece of newspaper and drop it into the bottom of the bottle so that no soil mix drains out of the bottom of the bottle (what used to be the top). Water will still be able to drain through.

Once you have the newspaper in the bottom of the bottle, fill the bottle with soil mix and either plant a few seeds or transplant an existing plant into the container.

APPENDIX C:
Step By Step Outdoor Gardening Build Plan

Step 1:
Observe the sun in your yard and find the sunniest 4' by 4' spot.

Step 2: Make sure that this spot is not in a low-lying spot in the yard. Annual plants do not do well with excess water. If you put a garden in a low spot, a few heavy rains can compromise your plants.

Step 3: Mark off the area. If you have time before the beginning of the planting schedule, put down organic material (compost, leaves, grass clippings) over the existing turf. Pile it as high as you care to then put cardboard over the pile. Tie cardboard down so that it doesn't blow away. Doing this will insulate the underlying soil from extreme low temperatures which will enable soil life to work its way up to the organic material and begin to break it down. No matter what kind of soil you have, this additional organic material will be beneficial.

Step 3a: If you don't have the time to allow for the slow breakdown of organic material (and we mean months when we say slow, not days or weeks), you have two options; dig up the existing soil or create a raised bed using soil from another place. To try to keep costs down, we recommend that you dig the area up and add some well-aged compost. If you are not sure where to purchase this, we recommend asking a local gardener in your area to find out the best local source. If this isn't possible, Home Depot and Lowe's both sell bags of compost. Keep in mind that you don't have to use anything to support your raised bed, if you build one. as long as it is more or less flat, not that much soil will run off. Putting leaves or straw on areas of open soil will help to prevent erosion as well.

Step 4: Mark off the 1 foot squares however you wish. If appearance isn't important, twine will do fine to mark the boundaries of the squares.

Step 5 (optional): Build and install wire garden towers (only along the north facing border of your garden to avoid shading the other squares). Instructions for building garden towers can be found in Appendix F.

Step 6: Make first planting according to schedule in Chapter 1.

Notes: If you use wood, do not use treated wood as it contains chemicals that will leech into the soil. Cedar is the classic wood to use for raised beds because it is slow to break down. Even other types of untreated wood will still last for at least a few years.

APPENDIX F:
Step By Step Wire Garden Tower Guide

In an effort to clarify some of the information from the 4 Foot Farm Guide, we have created this additional build guide so that you can follow along on a step by step process as a garden tower is constructed.

The materials used to build the tower are as follows:

- 3 feet tall fencing, 2 sections that are about 40" long each.
- 3 feet wide landscape cloth, 2 sections, 42" long each.
- zip ties and wire for assembly

Tools used:

- wire cutter
- pliers
- leather gloves

- box cutter
- measuring tape

Step 1: Count out 19 squares in the fencing, which when made into a cylinder, will be approximately 1 foot in diameter.

Step 2: Use the wire cutters to cut the fencing to the desired length.

Step 3: Count out 20 squares in the fencing.

Step 4: Use the wire cutters to cut the fencing.

Step 5: Form the cut fence into a cylinder.

Step 6: Hook the ends of the fence together the keep the cylinder in place.

Step 7: Check to make sure the cylinder is about 1 foot in diameter.

Step 8: Roll out and cut two lengths of 42" of landscape fabric with the box cutter.

Step 9: Place one of the sections inside the first cylinder you have constructed.

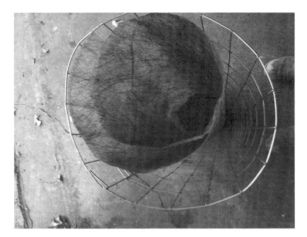

Step 10: Poke two holes in the fabric at one end of the cylinder, one on each side of one of the vertical wires in fence. Use a zip tie or a length of wire to fix the material into place. Make sure that the two holes pierce through the overlapped fabric as that will help hold the shape of the material. You can repeat this step at the other end, as well as on the other side of the cyclinder.

This first cylinder will be the "top" of the garden tower. Now that you have completed this section, set it aside.

Step 11: Repeat steps 5, 6 and 7 with the piece that is 20 squares long. When completing step 6 this time, leave the last two ends of the fence unwoven.

Step 12: Insert the top section of the garden tower (the one with the lining) into the bottom section. Overlap the sections by two rectangles.

Step 13: Weave the ends of the two fence sections together. In the pictures, you will see that I have lined the seams of the cylinders up. After thinking about it, it will be more stable to put the two seams on the opposite sides of the cylinders.

Step 14: Next, use some spare wire (or zip ties, but wire will be more sturdy) to secure the two sections of the cylinder together. Put these wires at 12, 3, 6 and 9 o'clock on the cylinders. I used my fingers and pliers to weave the wire around. You can do this in more places if you feel it is necessary. I do not think it is so important because the top of the garden tower will not be bearing a significant amount of weight.

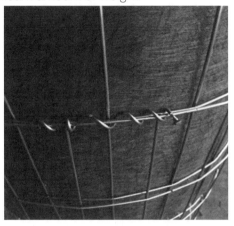

Step 15: Take the other length of landscape fabric and slide it into the bottom portion of the cylinder. This will take some doing, as there will not be a lot of space between the wires where the two cylinders overlap.

Step 16: With the second length of fabric in place, poke two holes in the fabric at the end of the cylinder, one on each side of one of the vertical wires in fence. Use a zip tie or spare wire to hold this in place. Repeat this step at the 6 o'clock position opposite where you just fixed the fabric to the cylinder.

Step 17: Now that you have the tower assembled, dig a hole about 8 inches deep and 16 inches wide, put the loose dirt from the hole in a bucket. Assuming you are building all four towers, dig four holes.

Step 18: Put the tower in the hole. Take the bucket of loose dirt from the hole and pour it carefully into the tower. Then backfill around the tower with the remaining loose dirt around the hole. Add some additional loose dirt around the bottom if necessary.

Step 19: Carefully fill the tower with potting soil. Make sure that the soil is not wet when you add it.

Step 20: When you are ready to transplant into the towers, cut an X into the fabric inside of one of the rectangles and pull the material back.

Step 21: Put the plant into the hole cut into the fabric.

Step 22: Once you have transplanted all plants into the tower, water from the top and along the sides through the fabric.

Don't be one of the 99.9% of people that enjoyed the guide yet don't leave us any positive feedback. Click the link below and let us know what you liked about the guide and you might just get a free gift. http://www.crisiseducation.com/content/customer-feedback/

OR

Visit our Facebook and leave us a comment at http://facebook.com/crisiseducation

Published by:
Crisis Education, LLC
4175 Freidrich Lane
Suite 202
Austin, TX 78744

Website: http://www.CrisisEducation.com
E-Mail: support@crisiseducation.com